Greater Than Prince Edward Island Canada

50 Travel Tips from a Local

Lorraine Rumson

Order Information: To order this title please email lbrenenc@gmail.com or visit GreaterThanATourist.com. A bulk discount can be provided.

Cover Template Creator: Lisa Rusczyk Ed. D. using Canva.
Cover Creator: Lisa Rusczyk Ed. D.
Image: https://pixabay.com/en/prince-edward-island-canada-54990/

Lock Haven, PA
All rights reserved.
ISBN: 9781549792335

>TOURIST

50 TRAVEL TIPS FROM A LOCAL

Lorraine Rumson

BOOK DESCRIPTION

Are you excited about planning your next trip?

Do you want to try something new?

Would you like some guidance from a local?

If you answered yes to any of these questions, then this Greater Than a Tourist book is for you.

Greater than a Tourist: Prince Edward Island by Lorraine Rumson offers the inside scoop on Prince Edward Island, Canada's smallest province. Most travel books tell you how to sightsee. Although there's nothing wrong with that, as a part of the Greater than a Tourist series, this book will give you tips from someone who lives at your next travel destination. In these pages, you'll discover local advice that will help you throughout your trip. Travel like a local. Slow down and get to know the people and the culture of a place. By the time you finish this book, you will be eager and prepared to travel to your next destination.

Lorraine Rumson

TABLE OF CONTENTS

9. Sip on an Island craft beer at Upstreet Craft Brewing

10. Make PEI your Thanksgiving destination

11. Explore the Charlottetown Farmer's Market

12. Sip on the famous "Charlottetown Fog"

13. Visit in September and walk in Charlottetown's AIDS Walk, a fundraiser for those living with HIV and AIDS

14. Pose for a historic picture at Grandpa's Antique Photo Studio

15. Sing with the sands at the Basin Head Beach

16. Want a dinner that fills you up without breaking the bank?

17. Feeling like a richer meal?

18. Stroll down Confederation Trail

19. Watch out for the jellyfish!

20. Visit in winter for a staggering snowfall

21. Absorb some Atlantic literary culture with the Winter's Tales Public Readings

22. Take in some up-and-coming talent with the University of Prince Edward Island's annual Creative Writing Master Class Showcase!

23. Scare yourself silly at Kensington's Haunted Mansion

24. Treat your taste buds at Mary's Bake Shoppe

25. Hike the trails at Bonshaw Hills Provincial Park

26. Forage for wild mushrooms in the woods

27. Swap out pub crawls for beach crawls!

28. Have an award-winning sushi platter at Ta-Ke Sushi!

29. Relax after a long day with Moonsnail's handcrafted incense and soaps

30. Appreciate Island Art at the Lorimer Gallery

31. Support artists from all across Canada when you attend Art in the Open

32. Learn about Acadian culture at Acadian Day

33. Discover PEI's forests with MacPhail Woods

34. Experience the past at Orwell Corner

35. Bike the heritage roads

36. Catch your own dinner when you go deep-sea fishing!

37. Fish at the docks instead, if that's more your speed

38. Relax by the water in an Adirondack chair

39. Support Island immigrants at Sadat's Cuisine

40. Pet the cutest of animals at Island Hill Farms

41. Catch a shave and a story or two at Ray's Place Barbershop

42. Play a game at the Small Print Board Game Café

DEDICATION

This book is dedicated to the fine and friendly folks of Prince Edward Island, without whom, this book would be very short.

Lorraine Rumson

ABOUT THE AUTHOR

Lorraine Rumson is a student of literature in Charlottetown, Prince Edward Island. She loves to read, dance, and sip lattes at the coffee shops of downtown Charlottetown, where she's lived for the past five years.

She loves to travel, and hopes to live in at *least* four different countries in her lifetime, but Charlottetown will always be her dream home.

Lorraine Rumson

HOW TO USE THIS BOOK

The Greater Than a Tourist book series was written by someone who has lived in an area for over three months. The goal of this book is to help travelers either dream or experience different locations by providing opinions from a local. The author has made suggestions based on her own experiences. Please do your own research before traveling to the area in case the suggested places are unavailable.

Lorraine Rumson

FROM THE PUBLISHER

Traveling can be one of the most important parts of a person's life. The anticipation and memories that you have are some of the best. As a publisher of the Greater Than a Tourist book series, as well as the popular 50 Things to Know book series, we strive to help you learn about new places, spark your imagination, and inspire you. Wherever you are and whatever you do I wish you safe, fun, and inspiring travel.

Lisa Rusczyk Ed. D.

CZYK Publishing

Lorraine Rumson

WELCOME TO > TOURIST

Lorraine Rumson

INTRODUCTION

Have you ever stood in the middle of a bustling city and wondered what it would be like to be in that same city half a century earlier? Do you long for a nostalgic past, where people cared about their neighbours, and helped strangers on the street?

If this describes you, then Prince Edward Island might be the place for you. Known as PEI, or simply "the Island" to locals, Canada's smallest province will have you feeling like you stepped into your grandma's stories about small-town life. The people are friendly and sociable. Businesses are locally-owned and locally-supported. The pace of life is relaxed, until the snowfall hits – when the whole Island bands together in the face of adversity!

It's easy to come to PEI and see the main tourist attractions – the famous Green Gables house, the historic museums, and the Confederation Centre, where Canada's status as a country was decided. But there's a whole lot more to it than that! I can help you find the best little-known attractions and amenities, the best snacks, and the best ways to spend your days when you just don't feel like seeing any other tourists around.

Visit PEI, and you will find yourself immersed in a world you probably thought never really existed. It's so familiar that you might just feel like you've been here before.

PEI

1. Book your trip during the low points in tourist season

Prince Edward Island is a hugely popular tourist destination! Unfortunately, that means that it can get pretty crazy during the "high season."

The biggest period for tourists is between Canada Day (July 1st) and Old Home Week (the middle of August). If you want a safer, less crowded, and more relaxed travel experience, try going to PEI in June, late August, or even September!

2. Avoid going during the winter

Unless you're a very brave soul, avoid travelling to PEI during the winter – and "winter" is between late November and May. During this time, you might get surprise snowstorms, or just terrible, cold weather! Besides, a lot of the attractions that might draw you to the Island will be closed, and you might not even be able to get a good fresh lobster supper! Instead, try to travel during the beautiful fall season (September through November) or the late spring or summer.

3. Relive your childhood love of Anne of Green Gables with the Anne of Green Gables musical

L. M. Montgomery's classic children's book *Anne of Green Gables* is one of the bestselling Canadian novels of all time. In 1956 (48 years after the original book was published), a musical version was made to be broadcast on CBC Television, Canada's premiere broadcasting company. In 1965, the stage version appeared in the Charlottetown Festival. It's been running every single year since, making it Canada's longest-running musical… and in 2014, it appeared in the Guinness Book of World Records as the longest running annual musical theatre production in the world!

4. Take it a step further, and go see Anne and Gilbert

The musical *Anne of Green Gables* is based on L. M. Montgomery's book of the same title, but did you know that there were sequels to that book? Two of them inspired the Victoria Playhouse, in the PEI town Victoria-by-the-Sea, to create a musical based on Anne's grown-up life! Today, it's being performed in downtown Charlottetown, at the local independent theatre, The Guild. The Guild has a tight space, so if you go see it there, get ready to have Anne *right* in front of you.

5. Visit The Guild for edgier theatre experiences

When Charlottetown isn't putting on musicals based on PEI's most famous book, it's putting on a huge range of other stage plays, dance troupes, and musical performances. Some of the recent performances include a musical called *Atlantic Blue*, which tells the story of how music arrived in Canada's east coast. There's also an improvised sketch comedy series called *Popalopalots*, regular showings of art in the basement, and, of course, the Charlottetown Burlesque team. If *Anne of Green Gables* is just a little too mainstream for you, The Guild is the place to go!

6. Step back in time by following the Confederation Players troupe around historic downtown Charlottetown

The Confederation Players are a group of historical actors who walk around downtown Charlottetown to bring history alive. They can take you on a walking tour around town and teach you all sorts of fun and colourful stories about the city. You can also find out what really happened when the country of Canada was formed, or watch some Victorians play a croquet game. Photo-ops with the Confederation Players are also a classic! Any Charlottetown traveler should get their picture taken with a couple of hoop-skirted ladies and top-hatted gentlemen!

7. Cool off with the world's best ice cream

That's right, Prince Edward Island is home to COWS Creamery – named number-one ice cream destination in the world by Tauck World Discovery! Their recipe is a family classic, shared around the turn of the century. It's made with real cream – not milk! – and comes in dozens of flavours. There are classics like chocolate and strawberry, and local delicacies like island blueberry. And if you're a sucker for great product names, you can also get yourself a scoop of "Messie Bessie" (chocolate with Oreo and toffee), "Wowie Cowie" (vanilla with English toffee marble and chocolate flakes), or "Fluff and Udder" (chocolate with marshmallow swirl and peanut butter cups).

8. Save money by sleeping at the University of Prince Edward Island

What's the point in going broke paying for an expensive hotel, if you're going to spend most of your days on the beach or in town? Fortunately, the University of Prince Edward Island opens up its dorm rooms every summer for a hotel operation! It's a slick, minimalist situation, with simple rooms that can fit up to four, and rock-bottom prices – even during the height of tourist season. And your neighbors could include the 500 Taiwanese monks, nuns, and followers, who chose PEI for a retreat this year!

9. Sip on an Island craft beer at Upstreet Craft Brewing

Upstreet Brewery is a nationally famous microbrewery with dozens of unique beers on tap. From the "Rhuby Social" Rhubarb Witbier, to the "Gravedigger Imperial Pumpkin Ale" (available only in the fall), there's sure to be something that suits your tastes! Not a drinker? Try their Day Drift Sodas, in unique flavours like apple-ginger-elderflower and strawberry-rhubarb-basil! It's the perfect way to cool off after a long hot summer day.

10. Make PEI your Thanksgiving destination

Of course, everyone wants to go to PEI in the summer – and it's gorgeous! But go for Thanksgiving, and you'll see trees in colours that you thought only existed in crayon boxes. You can also feast on farm-fresh turkey, crisp local apples, and squash that just came out of the ground! Bring your whole family for a holiday you won't soon forget.

"I'm so glad I live in a world where there are

Octobers"

– L. M. Montgomery, Anne of Green Gables

Lorraine Rumson

11. Explore the Charlottetown Farmer's Market

Twice a week, a farmer's market pops up across the street from the University of Prince Edward Islands – and Island farmers and artisans bring their A-game! There's fresh produce from not even two miles away. There are hand-crafted soaps, hand-carved decorations, and hand-knit sweaters. The Deep Roots Distillery even shows up with their collection of artisan liquors, from maple liqueur to genuine absinthe! And if you're feeling hungry, the farmer's market *the* place to go for lunch, with everything from mini-donuts made right in front of you, to heaping servings of fresh Chinese stir-fry.

12. Sip on the famous "Charlottetown Fog"

Sure, you *could* grab a coffee at Starbucks like you would in any other town. But wouldn't you rather walk just one block down Queen Street (Charlottetown's main street) and pick up a Charlottetown Fog instead? The Charlottetown Fog is the signature drink of The Kettle Black, PEI's 5-star coffee shop. It's like a London fog (i.e. a delicious earl grey vanilla latte), but absolutely everything in it – from the tea leaves to the vanilla syrup – is made locally!

13. Visit in September and walk in Charlottetown's AIDS Walk, a fundraiser for those living with HIV and AIDS

There are a lot of great things about PEI, but because it's so small, its health care resources leave a little to be desired! That's why PEI's PEERS Alliance (formerly AIDS PEI) runs the annual Scotiabank AIDS Walk. Every single dollar raised during the Walk stays on the Island, and it goes towards programs for improving the lives of people living with HIV and AIDS. So if you feel like doing some good, while also strolling through historical downtown Charlottetown on a beautiful fall day, this might be something you'd like to do!

14. Pose for a historic picture at Grandpa's Antique Photo Studio

Have you ever wished you were a dashing cowboy from the old west? How about a fine flapper, or a stylish Victorian lady? At Grandpa's Antique Photo Studio, you can live out those dreams! Take a step back in time with any one of seven different types of costumes, and eighteen scale sets. Dress up, pose with the set, and commemorate your historical moment forever! This is especially great for kids – is there *anything* cuter than a baby dressed as a '20s gangster? I think not.

15. Sing with the sands at the Basin Head Beach

The unique structure of the sand at PEI's Basin Head Beach has given it the name "the singing sands." When you walk across it, the sand squeaks, groans, and sings! Bring your whole family and put on a singing sands concert by dancing and rubbing your feet across the surface.

16. Want a dinner that fills you up without breaking the bank?

Go to Splendid Essence, an all-vegitarian Taiwanese restaurant, where you can get an amazing serving of bamboo rice with water chestnuts and tofu for just a couple dollars, and two servings' worth of noodles with rice for less than $10!

17. Feeling like a richer meal?

Treat yourself to a luxurious meal of butter chicken (or butter paneer, butter salmon, or even butter lobster!) at Himalayan Curry. There are other curries too – but the butter chicken is the best in the world! Its sister restaurant, Spicey Chef, shares most of its menu – but also serves cocktails, if you want a bit of a buzz to go with your curry.

18. Stroll down Confederation Trail

Confederation Trail is the original route of PEI's train tracks. There's no train on PEI anymore – it was abandoned in 1989. The tracks were removed to make the space into a gorgeous, 435 kilometer path! It's a low, rolling trail (no sharp hills to worry about) and links Charlottetown, Tignish, Montague, and even the Confederation Bridge. Whether you're walking or biking, whether you want to try to hike the whole Island (over the course of a few days, okay?) or just stroll from the Charlottetown Mall to the Harbour without walking down a main street, the Confederation Trail can't be missed!

19. Watch out for the jellyfish!

In July, PEI's waters swarm with jellies! They're mostly harmless, but they're pretty slimy, and they can completely cover the beaches in peak season. Don't go swimming in jelly-infested waters (some of them can give nasty stings, and you never know which ones they are!) but do check out the beaches... you'll never see so many jellyfish in your life!

20. Visit in winter for a staggering snowfall

Normally, I wouldn't recommend travelling to PEI in winter... but if you're truly interested in finding out what it's like to be buried under several meters of snow, you can try it! The average snowfall in PEI is around three meters over the whole winter, but 2015 saw a record-breaking *five and a half meters* of snow – about 18 feet. And lest you think that was just a freak accident, 2017 saw a record-breaking blizzard – 17.2 centimeters (about 7 inches) of snow in just one night!

"Canadians are fond of a good disaster, especially

if it has ice, water, or snow in it."

– Margaret Atwood

Lorraine Rumson

21. Absorb some Atlantic literary culture with the Winter's Tales Public Readings

Featuring writers, both well-known and obscure, from all across the Maritime region of Canada, Charlottetown's Winter's Tales program is committed to bringing the best of Atlantic literature to the Island. They host public readings of novel excerpts, memoirs, poetry, and even songs, all through the fall and winter seasons. Most of the readings are hosted either at the University, or at the Confederation Centre for the Arts or the Charlottetown Public Library. They're free, and always open to drop-ins!

22. Take in some up-and-coming talent with the University of Prince Edward Island's annual Creative Writing Master Class Showcase!

Is attending readings from renowned (published) writers just a little too mainstream for you? Once a year, in either November or April, the University of Prince Edward Island Creative Writing Master Class stages a public reading from a dozen of the top creative writing students! Both mature learners and undergrads perform at the Showcase, and the types of writing range from novel excerpts to memoirs to plays. Sometimes it's hosted in the 1880s Main Building of the University, and sometimes it's at a hip coffee shop downtown – keep an eye out for announcements!

23. Scare yourself silly at Kensington's Haunted Mansion

Overlooking the tiny town of Kensington, this Tudor-style mansion was said to have once been a boarding house known for sinister goings-on. Today, it's a haunted house experience that both kids and adults will love! There are paths that can lead you through either scary or not-so-scary rooms, so you never need to fear that your child (or you) will be left in tears... you can adjust the spookiness to your personal comfort level! But the real highlight is the spinning vortex hallway – I went through it eight years ago and still haven't forgotten the experience! It must be walked through to be believed.

24. Treat your taste buds at Mary's Bake Shoppe

So you've just finished going through the haunted mansion and are feeling a bit peckish… what to do? Fortunately, Kensington is also home to Mary's Bake Shoppe, a home-style bakery with five-star ratings! You can get fresh bread, homemade preserves, and delightful cookies, but the real star is the range of mouth-watering pies that they have to offer. Whether you love a lemon meringue or crave a coconut cream, Mary's Bake Shoppe will be able to satisfy you.

25. Hike the trails at Bonshaw Hills Provincial Park

Just off the Trans-Canada Highway, but like a whole other world! Bonshaw Hills has over 25 kilometers of hiking paths, both short, relaxed ones, and seriously challenging options, all connected to a main trail. Whether you want to hike or bike, you'll have no shortage of gorgeous scenery to enjoy while you inhale the fresh hill air. There's also a playground with a great swing-set and some picnic tables for a relaxed lunch. And here's a fun fact – the main trail is called Ji'ka'wa'katik Trail – Mi'kmaq for "the place where bass are plentiful."

26. Forage for wild mushrooms in the woods

Most of PEI is pretty cultivated – after all, people have been farming the fertile land for hundreds of years. But there are some pockets of wild forest still left, and if you're brave, you may just be able to find something delicious hiding in the underbrush. Do your research, though, and don't go eating anything you're not 100% confident about! Just finding it is treat enough.

27. Swap out pub crawls for beach crawls!

Sure, Charlottetown has a couple of great pubs, but be honest. Would you rather drop a couple hundred dollars in one night to get hammered and feel like garbage in the morning, *or*... would you rather swing from beach to beach, get a great tan, frolic in the waves, make memories with your friends, and pay not a cent more than the price of gas? I thought so! When there are so many beaches so close together, the 15-minute car trips from one to the next are totally worth it!

28. Have an award-winning sushi platter at Ta-Ke Sushi!

It may surprise you that Charlottetown has a great range of authentic Japanese food – since, well, it's a pretty "British Isles" city. But PEI is a hot destination for Japanese immigrants, as well as thousands of students from Japan at the internationally-oriented University! Ta-Ke Sushi serves a range of Korean dishes as well as classic sushi platters and Japanese staples like gyoza and miso soup. Thanks to Charlottetown's vibrant Japanese community, folks on the Island can enjoy the best of every world at this award-winning locally-owned operation!

29. Relax after a long day with Moonsnail's handcrafted incense and soaps

Walk into Moonsnail Soapworks, just off Queen Street, and you'll be greeted with a cloud of heavenly scents. Moonsnail carries everything Island-crafted, from pottery to hot sauce, but the real highlight are the gorgeous scented incenses and soaps. Of course, you can get classic scents like lavender and frankincense… but, if you're feeling a bit more adventurous, you can also get a soap in the scent of your favourite local beer from Upstreet Craft Brewing! Anything is possible.

30. Appreciate Island Art at the Lorimer Gallery

The Lorimer Gallery is located on Victoria Row, a street of historic buildings, including shops and restaurants, tucked into the bottom of Charlottetown. At the Lorimer Gallery, you can admire paintings, sculptures, and even jewellery created by local artists. Everything in the gallery speaks to the Canadian, especially Atlantic Canadian, experience, drawing on local traditions and culture as well as the gorgeous landscape. If you're an art lover, this gallery can't be missed!

"It is wonderful to feel the grandness of Canada in the raw"

– Emily Carr

Lorraine Rumson

31. Support artists from all across Canada when you attend Art in the Open

Maybe you're into art that's a little more avant-garde than what the Lorimer Gallery has to offer. You might be more at home attending Art in the Open, an annual festival displaying visual, street, and performance art. 2017's festival included a life-sized sculpture of Sputnik crushing a car, an "Existential Crisis Hotline" (where you can use a vintage phone to call someone who can help you with your philosophical problems), and a parade of crows walking and squawking from the heart of the city to the waterfront.

32. Learn about Acadian culture at Acadian Day

Acadian Day is August 15th, and it commemorates the culture of the Acadian people, French-speaking Canadians who were expelled from their home by the British in the 1750s. Acadian Day's PEI celebrations are all bilingual (English and French), with special guests from the Mi'kmaq Confederacy. It's the biggest annual opportunity to celebrate Acadian culture and educate people about what it really means. Acadian performers, a carnival, and even fireworks were all held in 2017, the biggest year yet, and future celebrations promise to be even more spectacular.

33. Discover PEI's forests with MacPhail Woods

If you want your kids to learn about the importance of conserving the forests, or maybe just want to enjoy a nature hike yourself, then MacPhail Woods can help you. They offer summer camps from ages 6 to 16 that teach children how to do everything from observe an insect to walk with a fox. There are also courses designed for adults, to educate you about PEI's natural ecosystems without making you feel like you're in high school biology class! And if you just want to enjoy the forest's splendor, you can enjoy the Native Plant Arboretum, or any one of the many specifically designed walking trails.

34. Experience the past at Orwell Corner

There are lots of ways to experience history in PEI, from visiting our museums to watching our Confederation Players! But if you really want to get down-and-dirty and find out what it was like to live in the 1800s, then you need to go to Orwell Corner. This historic village will immerse you in life in a two-hundred-year-old Atlantic village. Costumed guides will lead you through their daily activities like blacksmithing and candle-making. You'll leave with a renewed appreciation for everything we have today... but also with a little bit of longing for a time gone by!

35. Bike the heritage roads

PEI is criss-crossed with old dirt roads that you won't find on any modern map! An adventurous soul can take a bike through the woods and ride for hours, experiencing whole different worlds. Stay safe, and make sure that both you and some other people know where you are. It's easy to get lost... but getting just a *little* bit lost is part of the experience.

36. Catch your own dinner when you go deep-sea fishing!

You can book a fishing tour that will take you out onto the open ocean to go after some game! Whether you're interested in catching tuna or lobster, feeling your capture tug on your line (or boat!) will give you a whole new understanding of what seafood is. Some wranglings with tuna have been known to last three hours or more! You can even scope out the sharks that lurk below the surface (nice and far away from the shore – no need for beachgoers to be alarmed).

37. Fish at the docks instead, if that's more your speed

Maybe you don't want to get on a fishing boat and wrestle with a giant tuna for three hours. That's okay! You can also choose to bring your fishing rod to Charlottetown's boardwalk, and try your luck on the slippery little fellows that dart up close to the city. Be prepared for some cheers from onlookers any time you pull a fish up out of the water!

38. Relax by the water in an Adirondack chair

Charlottetown has a whole row of Adirondack chairs (also known as "the comfiest chairs possible to make out of just wood") right on the dock! You'll be just a few feet from the water, can watch the ships come and go, and keep an eye on those dock fishers. I can confirm that this is the absolute *best* place in the city to sit and read.

39. Support Island immigrants at Sadat's Cuisine

PEI welcomes people from all nations. But it can be hard for new immigrants to make a business thrive in a town that can be a little shy on jobs and cash. You can help, while also enjoying the very best in Afghani and Middle Eastern food, by visiting Sadat's Cuisine downtown. It's a family-run establishment, and you can feel confident that you're supporting good people when you eat there. That's one of the best things about PEI – with so many local businesses, you can know that you're giving your business to people who truly appreciate it!

40. Pet the cutest of animals at Island Hill Farms

The Island has no shortage of farm animals… but few are as truly adorable as the baby goats, bunnies, and the sweet blind alpaca that are the stars of Island Hill Farm. It's a combination of a petting zoo and an educational opportunity – come visit the animals, hug and pet them, and also learn about life on a farm! Day cares and schools *love* doing trips to the Farm.

Island Hill Farm was voted one of the most-loved small businesses of Canada in a study run by the Canadian Federation of Independent Business.

"It's the ordinary things that seem important to me"

– Alex Coville

Lorraine Rumson

41. Catch a shave and a story or two at Ray's Place Barbershop

Sometimes, you need a great haircut. Sometimes you also need someone great to talk to. You can get both of these when you visit Ray's Place Barbershop. It'll have you feeling like you've stepped into an old movie where barbers dispense wisdom while they work. Just sit back, relax, and take in a couple of anecdotes about goings-on on the Island.

42. Play a game at the Small Print Board Game Café

Uno! Sorry! And/or Jenga! Small Print Board Game Café is open late into the evening, every day of the week, and provides an array of board and card games that you can stay and play while indulging in coffee, alcohol, or delicious snacks. Keep an eye out for special events, like trivia nights, or free stay-and-play opportunities!

43. Zoom down the Summerside Board Walk on a Segway

Did you think Segway tours were only for big European cities that no one could get around on foot? Think again! You *could* walk down Summerside's scenic boardwalk… but you could also enjoy a guided tour of it while gliding along on a Segway. Perfect if you've spent the last few days hiking and your legs are worn out! You'll learn history, anecdotes, and how to balance safely on a Segway, all at the same time!

44. Find Eckhart the mouse in downtown Charlottetown

Inspired by David Weale's famous mouse explorer, Eckhart, Charlottetown has hidden nine tiny bronze mice all around the city. They're hiding in nooks and crannies all around the historic downtown area! Both children and children-at-heart can have an adventure, seeking out the nine little mice while you go on your other adventures around town.

45. Pound your friends at Crossfire Paintball

You might think that Prince Edward Island is all sweet pastoral farms and fishing boats. We have lots of those... but we also have paintball fields that are realistic recreations of Second World War battlefields. Crossfire Paintball is open seven days a week all summer, and then weekends until the middle of October. There are eight different fields, from a "D-Day Beach" to rows of trenches, this is one thing in this book that's sure to get your blood pumping.

46. Bounce "Off the Wallz" at Summerside's trampoline park

Trampolines aren't just for kids! At Off the Wallz trampoline park, the young-at-heart of all ages can bounce to their heart's content. They have a classic trampoline park, a soft play area perfect for kids, and even a splash park for the more water-inclined! Whether you want to jump off a trampoline to hit a slam dunk in the basketball section, or simply bounce off every imaginable surface, Off the Wallz guarantees such a good time that you won't even notice the workout you're getting... until the next day!

47. Place a prize pumpkin on the scales

Are you a squash-grower? Think you have what it takes to compete with Prince Edward Island's biggest pumpkins? Enter (or just stop by to observe) the annual pumpkin weigh-in. 2016's winner was more than 600 kilograms – or over 1,300 pounds! That's only a little bit lighter than a Smart Car. If you think you have a pumpkin that can compete (or just want your eyes to widen and your mouth to water at the thought of that much pumpkin pie), then you *must* watch the pumpkin weigh-ins.

48. Pick some farm-fresh apples

There's no shortage of apple orchards on the Island, but Arlington Orchards are the undisputed king, with 27 different types of apple, and 32 acres of dedicated land! The staff at Arlington Orchards are all trained specifically in the art of apples. Whether you go on the "U-pick" adventure of choosing your own, or you're just picking some up at the farmer's market, they'll ensure that you have the perfect apples for your cooking, eating, or preserving pleasure.

49. Sample all of PEI's fries

Did you know that Prince Edward Island is home to the McKay French Fry factory? That's because, in addition to being the lobster capital of Canada, PEI has world-famous potato farms! But when you're in Charlottetown, you don't need to confine yourself to frozen fries. Almost every restaurant in town has their own unique take on the french fry experience... and most for just a couple dollars, or less! Can you say "french fry crawl"? Who needs alcohol when you have fries!

50. Take an amphibious adventure in the Harbour Hippo

Finally, no trip to the Island would be complete without a ride on Charlottetown's Harbour Hippo! This unique bus will take you all over the city, while your tour guide tells you about the history, culture, and events of the town. Then, after you've done all you can do on land... the Harbour Hippo drives right into the ocean! That's right, this massive bus is actually a boat on wheels, and will take you for a spin around the waterfront, so you can experience Prince Edward Island by land *and* by sea.

Top Reasons to Book This Trip

- **The Beaches:** First thing's first: PEI's beaches are the best in Canada, hands-down. There's nowhere else in the country with such an awesome variety of swimmable locations.

- **The Food:** You'll never get such a wide variety of locally-owned restaurants in such a small space of real estate as in Charlottetown! Thanks to the awesome tourist population, small businesses can *stay* in business, catering to every palate imaginable.

- **The Island Culture:** While the food is delicious, and the beaches are fun, the real reason to come to PEI is to enjoy its uniquely kind culture. Maybe it's that we're all tied together by the shared experience of brutal winters. Maybe there's just something in the air. But you'll never meet friendlier folks than the Islanders.

Lorraine Rumson

> TOURIST

GREATER THAN A TOURIST

Visit GreaterThanATourist.com
http://GreaterThanATourist.com

Sign up for the Greater Than a Tourist Newsletter
http://eepurl.com/cxspyf

Follow us on Facebook:
https://www.facebook.com/GreaterThanATourist

Follow us on Pinterest:
http://pinterest.com/GreaterThanATourist

Follow us on Instagram:
http://Instagram.com/GreaterThanATourist

Lorraine Rumson

> TOURIST

GREATER THAN A TOURIST

Please leave your honest review of this book on Amazon and Goodreads. Thank you.

We appreciate your positive and negative feedback as we try to provide tourist guidance in their next trip from a local.

> TOURIST

GREATER THAN A TOURIST

Our Story

Traveling is a passion of the "Greater than a Tourist" series creator. Lisa studied abroad in college, and for their honeymoon Lisa and her husband toured Europe. During her travels to Malta, an older man tried to give her some advice based on his own experience living on the island since he was a young boy. She was not sure if she should talk to the stranger but was interested in his advice. When traveling to some places she was wary to talk to locals because she was afraid that they weren't being genuine. Through her travels, Lisa learned how much locals had to share with tourists. Lisa created the "Greater Than a Tourist" book series to help connect people with locals. A topic that locals are very passionate about sharing.

Lorraine Rumson

> TOURIST

GREATER THAN A TOURIST

Notes

Made in United States
Troutdale, OR
09/26/2023

13216615R00054